Lisa D. Hoff

CHARLESTON

SOUTH CAROLINA

Sightseeing in 88 Pictures.

in cooperation with

THE PRESERVATION SOCIETY OF CHARLESTON

CHARLESTON — *Past and Present.*

In April 1670, the frigate *Carolina*, with a group of British settlers, sailed into the harbor formed by the Cooper and Ashley (then called Kiawah) rivers. They built their first settlement on a low bluff overlooking Old Towne Creek.

The expedition, which had been at sea for seven months and had lost two ships, had been financed by the True and Absolute Lord Proprietors of Carolina. The Proprietors were eight politically powerful Englishmen who held a charter from the Crown granting them the lands stretching from North Carolina into Florida and westward to the South Seas.

The settlers included twenty-nine "masters" (men of property) and "free" persons, and sixty-three indentured white servants who had to serve their owners for two to seven years in return for the passage to Carolina, and one or two black slaves. The new settlement soon attracted boatloads of free men and indentured servants from the West Indies and England.

Some of the settlers, attracted by the wooded peninsula and the cooler breezes of a site across the Ashley, called White Point or Oyster Point because of the discarded oyster shells left there by the Indians, decided to build there. Charles Town's population increased rapidly, helped by the proprietors who hoped that by advertising Charles Town as being especially healthy and tolerant to all religions they could attract more immigrants who in turn would stimulate the economy and make Charles Town the premier trading harbor with England.

In the mid-1690s Charles Town was beginning to export rice, which had been imported from Madagascar ten years earlier. This crop was to make some of the planters and merchants the richest men in America. However, the planting, hoeing and harvesting of rice required strong laborers who were immune to malaria and yellow fever. Hundreds of West African slaves arrived in Charles Town each year.

Between 1712 and 1718 Charles Town and its inhabitants were in turn plagued by smallpox and yellow fever, followed by a big hurricane which lasted for twelve hours. When the effects of the hurricane leveled off, the Yamassee Indian War broke out and Indian raiding parties came within a few miles of the walls of Charles Town. When trading after the war started again, pirates seized the ships and plundered their cargo.

In early 1719 the Proprietors disallowed certain import duties passed by the Assembly, prohibited further issuance of money, and ended the policy of granting land to settlers, claiming for themselves the vast lands taken from the Yamassees, and requested the dissolution of the Assembly and a call for new elections. When news arrived in Charles Town that a Spanish armada was being readied to invade Carolina, the Assembly declared itself the new government under His Majesty's protection. Thus ended proprietory government in South Carolina.

The first twenty years of the new Royal Colony were prosperous years. Annually, over 500 oceangoing vessels docked at the eight wharves jutting into the Cooper River.

However, the 1740s brought a slave revolt, nine years of war in Europe, which disrupted the export trade, and the Great Fire of 1740 which destroyed about 300 houses and several wharves and fortifications. After the war, trade resumed with a vengeance. The planters of the lowcountry could not plant enough of the newly introduced crop indigo to satisfy the demand for the dye by England's fast-growing textile industry.

By the 1760s and early 1770s the value of Carolina crops soared, and the annual export-import trade exceeded even the

tonnage through New York's port. Well-to-do Charlestonians built grand, new houses, the ladies wore the latest London fashions to the theater, to balls and concerts and bought their furniture from Thomas Elfe. Their sons were educated abroad or by private teachers. Three newspapers and the only bookstore and bindery in the South kept the people of Charles Town informed. The port's reputation for being wealthy and unhealthy attracted many physicians, several of whom were Scottish-born and educated, like Alexander Garden, a botanist for whom the gardenia is named, or Lionel Chalmers, who undertook studies of tetanus and meteorology.

On June 28, 1776, while delegates to the Continental Congress in Philadelphia were still debating the issue of separation from the mother country, nine British warships attacked the fort on Sullivan's Island but were forced to retreat. Charles Town was saved. Four months later, the government of Charles Town approved the Declaration of Independence. With the war concentrating in the northeastern states, which interrupted the trade through Boston, New York and Philadelphia, more ships than ever before docked in Charles Town. In 1779, the British, unable to win a decisive battle over Washington's armies, and hoping that an invasion of the South would disrupt the trade, sent a massive combined sea and land expedition to Charles Town. After a 42-day siege America's last open seaport had to surrender. The occupation of Charles Town lasted for two and a half years.

In 1783 the South Carolina legislature dramatically announced the city's new independence from the British Crown by changing the name to Charleston. Three years later they voted over the vigorous opposition of the lowcountry delegation to move the state capital inland to a site that was eventually named Columbia.

Around the turn of the century a new crop was fast replacing rice and indigo in the export trade. In 1791 South Carolina grew 1.5 million pounds of cotton, a decade later 20 million, and production doubled again within the next ten years. After the Napoleonic Wars the demand for cotton in Europe soared and planters rushed to spend their money on Sea Island mansions and summer homes in the city.

The Medical College of South Carolina opened in 1824 as the South's first school of medicine. A military school, the Citadel, was chartered in 1842. A free public school reformed Charleston's school system into the best in South Carolina.

New rail lines connected Charleston with Hamburg, Louisville, Cincinnati, Memphis and Savannah. Charleston became the manufacturing center of South Carolina with numerous rice and grist mills, iron foundries, turpentine distilleries, saw mills, different factories, and a railroad depot and machine shop. The inequality in the distribution of wealth in the city was enormous; some 3% of the population owned approximately half of all the wealth.

In December 1860, 169 delegates convened in Columbia to vote on secession. The outbreak of smallpox forced the Secession Convention to move to Charleston where they voted 169 : 0 to secede from the Union. Following the formation of the Confederate States of America at Montgomery, Alabama, President Jefferson Davis ordered General Beauregard to take charge of the volatile situation in Charleston. Major Anderson, who had moved his Federal troops to strategically important Fort Sumter, refused to surrender, and the first shots of the Civil War were fired onto Fort Sumter. For nearly four years Charleston stood defiant in the face of a relentless Federal siege from the sea. When, at last, on the night of February 17, 1865, the Confederate troops finally evacuated their positions, and the city of Charleston fell, it was because Sherman's troops were threatening the state's capital and Charleston's supply lines. Charleston was a city of ruins and desolation.

Economic recovery was slow, but, little by little, the destroyed rail lines and burnt-out sections of the city were rebuilt. Charleston's economy received a boost with the discovery by two scientists at the College of Charleston that phosphate deposits found in the river banks could be used in the manufacturing of fertilizer.

The last quarter of the 19th century saw big changes. The harbor was modernized; the first telephones were installed; new contraptions, called bicycles, and electric trolley cars made the city easily accessible; the crushed shells covering city streets were replaced with flagstones and granite; and finally the city started with its most ambitious and urgent project: replacing the unhealthy privy system with a modern sewage system. Fertilizer factories, saw mills, a cotton factory and sheetmetal works provided jobs, and good profits were made in the crab/shrimp 'industry' and produce farming for northern markets.

In 1920 some farsighted Charlestonians launched the first preservation movement. The Society for the Preservation of Old Dwellings, later changed to the Preservation Society of Charleston, saved many landmarks from destruction. In 1931 the city of Charleston adopted the first Planning and Zoning Ordinance to protect the historic district.

The transition from an era of segregation to one of equality under the law was a stormy one, but thanks to farsighted black and white leaders, Charleston was the first city in South Carolina to integrate public high schools, municipal facilities, the police force and other city jobs.

In the last twenty years port activity has expanded rapidly; Charleston has become the number-one containership port on the East Coast. Hundreds of houses have been restored, a new Charleston Museum has been built, and the city has acquired tourist attractions such as Cypress Gardens and Charles Towne Landing. The central business district has been rejuvenated with the construction of Charleston Place, and the Spoleto Festival annually attracts numerous art and music lovers from all over the world. In November 1985, *US News and World Report* selected Charleston from seventy-four metropolitan areas as the city "where business is best."

Shortly before midnight on September 21, 1989, Hurricane Hugo, with winds up to 135 mph, and pushing a 12- to 17-foot wall of water, roared into Charleston and the surrounding coastal areas. The barrier islands were inundated. Charleston had to be evacuated; trees were uprooted; slate, tin and copper roofs were blown away; chimneys and garden walls collapsed; glass store fronts exploded; and the water pouring through the streets covered everything up to the first floor with mud. Like so often in its 300 years of history, Charleston rallied together the next day and started rebuilding.

Die Geschichte der Stadt Charleston

Im April 1670 segelte das Schiff "Carolina" mit einer Gruppe von Auswanderern aus England kommend in den jetzigen Hafen von Charleston. Ihre erste Siedlung errichteten sie auf einer Anhöhe oberhalb des Ashley Flusses. Die Expedition, die sieben Monate unterwegs war, war von acht englischen Adeligen finanziert worden. Diese einflussreichen Persönlichkeiten hatten das Gebiet zwischen Nordkarolina und Florida von König Charles II für die ihm erwiesenen Dienste erhalten.

Zehn Jahre später verlegten die Ansiedler ihre Siedlung auf die Halbinsel zwischen dem Cooper und dem Ashley Fluss und nannten sie Charles Town. Die Bevölkerung von Charles Town wuchs schnell, angelockt durch die viel gepriesene Religionsfreiheit. Von Frankreich kamen Hugenotten, von England, den Westindischen Inseln, Schottland und Irland kamen Quäker, Presbyterianer, Baptisten und Juden. Heute noch sind in Charleston über 181 Kirchen, und es wird oft die "Heilige Stadt" genannt. Mitte 1690 begann Charles Town Reis in grossen Mengen nach England zu exportieren. Da der Reisanbau sehr arbeitsintensiv war und der Reis nur von Arbeitern angebaut werden konnte, die immun gegen Malaria und Gelbfieber waren, wurden mehr und mehr Sklaven aus Westafrika eingeführt. Als Krieg zwischen England und Frankreich ausbrach, drängten die aristokratischen Landbesitzer darauf, die Stadt zu befestigen. Um 1704 wohnten 3.500 Leute dicht gedrängt innerhalb der Stadtmauern.

Eine ständige Gefahr für die Bewohner Charles Towns waren ausser Feuer, Orkanen und Sklavenaufständen die immer wieder auftretenden Seuchen, besonders Pocken und Gelbfieber.

Empört über unzureichenden Schutz, unfaire Gesetze und Gleichgültigkeit von Seiten der adeligen Landbesitzer brachte 1719 die Versammlung (Assembly) von Charles Town eine Petition zur Abschaffung der adeligen Landbesitzer ein und bat um königlichen Schutz. Damit wurde Südkarolina eine königliche Kolonie. Zu diesem Zeitpunkt war Charles Town ein blühender Seehafen. Über 500 Schiffe legten pro Jahr an den acht Kaianlagen entlang des Cooperflusses an, um Luxusartikel, Weine und Sklaven zu entladen und Reis und Indigo für die englischen Märkte zu laden. Charles Town wurde die reichste und viertgrösste Stadt in Kolonialamerika. Die Kaufleute und Pflanzer legten ihr Geld in immer grösseren Plantagen, mehr Sklaven und eleganteren Stadthäusern an. Da Malaria im Sommer eine grosse Gefahr war, verbrachten die meisten Pflanzer mit ihren Familien diese Jahreszeit in der Stadt. Zur Unterhaltung veranstalteten sie Bälle, besuchten Konzerte, Theatervorstellungen oder trafen sich auf den Rennplätzen beim Pferderennen. Die Söhne wurden zur Ausbildung nach England und Schottland geschickt.

Obwohl die Stadt als königliche Kolonie Wohlstand erreichte, führte unfaire Besteuerung zu Widerstand gegen die königliche Oberherrschaft. Während die Delegierten beim Kontinentalen Kongress in Philadelphia 1776 noch darüber debattierten, ob man sich von England trennen sollte, griffen neun englische Kriegsschiffe die Befestigungsanlage auf der Insel Sullivan an. Die Briten wurden zurückgetrieben und das Fort nach seinem Kommandanten Fort Moultrie genannt. Vier Monate später stimmte die Regierung in Charles Town der Unabhängigkeitserklärung zu.

Während sich die Kriegshandlungen im Nordosten Amerikas abspielten, war Charles Town der einzige offene Hafen an der Ostküste. 1779 wurde jedoch Charles Town von den Briten besetzt. Die zweiein-halb Jahre dauernde Besetzung hinterliess tiefe Spuren in der Stadt. Die Stadtteile, die nicht von den Briten beschossen und geplündert worden waren, wurden zum Teil von Feuer zerstört. 1783 wurde die neue Unabhängigkeit dramatisch mit einem neuen Namen für die Stadt angekündigt. Charleston blieb noch drei Jahre die Hauptstadt Südkarolinas. 1786 stimmte die Mehrzahl der gesetzgebenden Versammlung dafür, die Hauptstadt ins Zentrum des Staates zu verlegen und Columbia wurde gegründet.

Ein neues landwirtschaftliches Produkt verdrängte bald den Reis- und Indigoanbau. 1791 wurden in Südkarolina ca. 1,5 Millionen Pfund Baumwolle angebaut, zehn Jahre später waren es 20 Millionen und 1811 40 Millionen. Für Charleston begann die anmutige Antebellum Zeit. Neue Eisenbahnlinien stellten die Verbindung mit dem Hinterland her, und Charleston wurde ein Industriezentrum.

Es dauerte jedoch nicht lange, und die wirtschaftliche Entwicklung kam zum Stillstand. 1860 trat Südkarolina aus den Vereinigten Staaten aus und bildete mit sieben anderen Südstaaten die Konföderierten Staaten von Amerika. Am 12. April 1861 wurden die ersten Schüsse des Bürgerkrieges von der Konföderierten Armee vom Fort Johnson auf das Fort Sumter abgegeben, das von den Unionsstreitkräften besetzt worden war.

Vier Jahre lang hielt Charleston einem föderalistischen Seeangriff stand. Die konföderierten Streitkräfte gaben erst auf und evakuierten die Stadt, als General Sherman Columbia und somit die Nachschublinie besetzte. Charleston lag in Ruinen. Der Wiederaufbau ging nur langsam vor sich, allerdings erhielt die Wirtschaft durch die Entdeckung, dass Phosphatablagerungen in den Flüssen sich zur Herstellung von Düngemitteln besonders gut eignen, einen Aufschwung. Kurz nach der Jahrhundertwende wurde der Hafen zum bedeutendsten Flottenstützpunkt an der Ostküste ausgebaut. 1920 gründeten einige vorausblickende Bürger die "Gesellschaft zur Erhaltung alter Wohnhäuser", die jetzt unter dem Namen "Preservation Society" bekannt ist. In den letzten zwanzig Jahren ist der Charleston Hafen zum bedeutendsten Containerhafen an der Ostküste herangewachsen. Hunderte von Häusern wurden restauriert, ein neues Museum eröffnet und die Spoletofestspiele locken jeden Sommer Tausende von Musik- und Kunstliebhabern aus aller Welt nach Charleston. Kurz vor Mitternacht am 21. September 1989 fiel Orkan "Hugo" über Charleston und die umliegenden Inseln herein. Bäume wurden entwurzelt, Dächer abgedeckt, Häuser und Kamine stürzten ein und eine 5 Meter hohe Wassermauer, die der Sturm vor sich hertrieb bedeckte Strassen, Eingänge und Gärten mit braunem Schlamm. Aber wie so oft in seinem 300-jährigen Bestehen liess sich Charleston mit seinen Bewohnern nicht unterkriegen. Mit Entschlossenheit und Mut fingen sie am nächsten Tag an, die Stadt wiederaufzubauen.

L'Histoire de Charleston

En avril 1670, le vaisseau "Caroline" avec un groupe d'immigrants anglais entra dans le port de Charleston. Les immigrants construirent leur première colonie sur une colline au-dessus de la rivière Ashley. L'expédition, en route pendant sept mois, fut financée par huit Seigneurs anglais. Ces personnages importants avaient reçu du roi Charles II, pour services rendus, le territoire qui s'étend de la Floride à la Caroline du Nord.

Dix ans plus tard ils décidèrent de construire une nouvelle colonie à l'endroit où la rivière Ashley se joint à la rivière Cooper et l'appelèrent Charles Town. La population de Charles Town grandit rapidement, attirée par des assurances de liberté religieuse. De France arrivaient des Huguenots, d'Angleterre, d'Ecosse, d'Ireland et des Antilles venaient, des Anglicans, des Quakers, des Presbytériens, des Baptistes et de Juifs. Aujourd'hui il y a encore plus de 180 églises à Charleston qui est souvent appelée "la Ville Sainte".

En 1695, Charles Town commença à exporter de grandes quantités de riz. Comme la culture du riz exige beaucoup de travail dur sous des conditions malsaines, les planteurs importèrent de plus en plus d'esclaves d'Afrique.

Quand la guerre éclata entre l'Angleterre et la France les propriétaires exigèrent que la ville soit entourée de fortifications. En 1704, 3.500 habitants se serraient entre ses murailles.

En plus des feux, des ouragans at des révoltes d'esclaves, la population de Charles Town fut constamment menacée d'épidémies, surtout de la variole et de la fièvre jaune.

Dégouté du manque de protection, des lois injustes et de l'insensibilité de la part des propriétaires, l'Assemblé de Charles Town présenta une petition au roi d'abolir le droit de propriété. En 1720 la Caroline du Sud devint une colonie royale.

Charles Town était un port fleurissant. Chaque année plus de 500 navires entraient dans le port pour décharger des articles de luxe, des vins et des esclaves et pour embarquer du riz et de l'indigo destinés aux marchés anglais. Charles Town devint la ville la plus riche d'Amérique.

Les marchands et les planteurs investirent dans des plantations de plus en plus grandes, ce qui exigea l'importation accélérée d'esclaves. Plus que la moitié de la population de Charles Town fut des esclaves. Comme la malaria fut prévalente, la plupart de planteurs et leurs familles passèrent l'été dans leurs maisons de ville. Pour se divertir, ils allaient aux bals, aux concerts, au théâtre et au courses de chevaux. Les fils étaient éduqués en Angleterre ou en Ecosse, les filles passaient une année de pensionnat à Charleston ou à Baltimore.

Des taxations injustes amenaient les colonies américaines à se révolter contre le Roi et le Parlement anglais. Pendant que les délégués au Congrès Continental à Philadelphie discutaient de la séparation avec l'Angleterre, neuf navires de guerre anglais attaquèrent l'île Sullivan à l'entrée du port de Charles Town. Après la première victoire de la Révolution américaine le fort fut nommé Fort Moultrie d'après son commandant. Quatre mois après, les délégués, dont quatre étaient de Charles Town, signèrent la Déclaration d'Indépendance. Pendant la Révolution Charles Town fut le seul port des États-Unis qui resta ouvert. En 1776, l'armée anglais occupa Charles Town. Après l'occupation, qui dura deux ans et demi la moitié de Charles Town fut détruite.

En 1783, Charles Town devint Charleston. Trois ans plus tard la législature décida d'établir une nouvelle capitale, Columbia, au centre de Caroline du Sud.

Un nouveau produit commençait à prendre la place du riz et de l'indigo. En 1781, la Caroline plantait à peu près 1.5 millions livres de coton, dix ans plus tard c'était 20 millions et en 1811 40 millions. Pour Charleston commença la période Antebellum avec ses maisons élégantes. Des chemins de fer liaient Charleston à d'autre villes, et elle devenait bientôt le centre industriel du sud.

Malheureusement ce boom ne dura pas longtemps. En 1860, la Caroline du Sud, à cause de la question de l'esclavage, sortit de l'union des États-Unis et forma avec les sept états du Sud les Etats Confédérés d'Amérique. Le 12 avril 1861, l'armée confédérée tirait le premier coup de feu de la guerre civile sur les troupes unionistes à Fort Sumter. Pendant, quatre ans Charleston résista aux attaques maritimes de la marine fédéraliste. A la fin de la guerre Charleston se retrouva en ruines.

La reconstruction fut longue et dure. La demande du coton sur le marchés europeens diminuait, et seule la découverte que les dépots de phosphate dans les rivières autour de Charleston produisaient des fertilisants sauva l'économie de Charleston.

En 1920, quelques Charlestoniens prévoyants créèrent la "Société pour Préserver les Vielles Maisons". Depuis lors la Sociéte de Préservation a sauvé des centaines de maisons de la destruction.

Aujourd'hui Charleston attire des visiteurs du monde entier avec ses belles maisons, son climat tempéré et surtout le Festival de Spoleto. Le 21 septembre 1989, vers minuit l'ouragan "Hugo" se lançait sur Charleston et les îles voisines. Il arracha des arbres et des toits, renversa des murs et des cheminées et couvra les rues et les premiers étages des maisons d'eau sale. Mais le lendemain, comme à plusieurs reprises dans ses 300 ans d'existence, Charleston reprit ses forces et recommença sa reconstruction.

Acknowledgements:

My special thanks are due to:
The Preservation Society of Charleston
Mrs. Helga Vogel
South Carolina Division of Tourism
The Charleston Trident Chamber of Commerce
Mr. and Mrs. Jean-Michel Bock
Mr. Wilson F. Fullbright
Spoleto Festival U.S.A.
The Charleston Museum of Art
The Gibbes Museum of Art

Photo Credit:
Charleston Museum of Art (46, 47b)
Charleston Post Card Company (5)
Gibbes Museum of Art (37)
Anne-Christine Hoff (7, 9, 29, 39, 44, 49)
Richard Lubrant (3b, 10, 11, 59, 62, 64)
John W. Meffert (14, 21a, 40, 52, 53)
Spoleto Festival U.S.A., William H. Struhs (54)
South Carolina Division of Tourism
Stills/Atlanta, Bill Weems (8)
The Abby Aldrich Rockefeller Folk Art Center,
  Williamsburg, VA (34)

Art Credit:
Elisabeth Hoff

City Hall, 80 Broad Street, built 1800-1801, open to the public. Designed by Gabriel Manigault, a Charleston planter/architect. This Adam-style building occupies the northeastern corner of the "Four Corners of Law," opposite the Charleston County Courthouse.

St. Michael's Episcopal Church, built 1752-1761. The oldest religious building in Charleston. The bells have crossed the Atlantic five times; they were imported from England in 1764, returned there as spoils of the Revolutionary War, were bought by a London merchant and shipped back, then were sent to England for recasting after they melted during the burning of Columbia where they had been sent for safekeeping

Nathaniel Russell House, 51 Meeting Street, built c.1808, open to the public. It was built by one of the wealthiest merchants of Charleston. The interior contains the famous "flying" staircase, the furnishings are of the period.

Calhoun Mansion, 16 Meeting Street, open to the public. The 35-room mansion, built in 1876, is considered to be one of the most important Victorian houses on the East Coast.

White Point Gardens, so named by the first settlers for the discarded oyster shells the Indians had left there. In 1718 Stede Bonnet, the gentleman pirate, and twenty-nine of his men were hanged at White Point.

Battery

South Battery

DeSaussure House, 1 East Battery, private residence. Built around 1858 by a Sea Island planter. From its wide piazzas, South Carolinians watched and cheered the bombardment of Fort Sumter in 1861.

East Battery as viewed from the sea.

John Ravenel House, 5 East Battery, private residence, built around 1847. This house was the home of Dr. St. Julien Ravenel, a doctor, planter and scientist who designed a 50-foot long, cigar-shaped torpedo boat, the "Little David," which helped open a new chapter in naval warfare.

Edmondston-Alston House, 13 East Battery, open to the public. Charles Edmonston, merchant and wharf owner, built this house c.1828. Ten years later it was bought by Colonel Charles Alston, a wealthy rice planter from Georgetown. The Alston family coat of arms still decorates the parapet. Contains a beautiful library and a large collection of Alston family furnishings.

East Battery

Stoll's Alley, several of the houses in Stoll's Alley are pre-Revolutionary.

George Eveleigh House, 39 Church Street, private residence, built in 1743 by a wealthy fur trader.

Ornamental ironwork is a Charleston tradition.

The poinsettia was named for Charlestonian Joel Poinsett.

The Art of lowcountry basket making was brought here from West Africa.

Heyward-Washington House, 87 Church Street, open to the public. Built c.1770. Was the home of Thomas Heyward, a signer of the Declaration of Independence. In 1791 President Washington stayed here during his tour of the nation. Good example of a Charleston double house with four rooms to the floor and a central stairway.

Cabbage Row, 89-91 Church Street. This tenement, built before the Revolutionary War, inspired DuBose Heyward's Catfish Row in his novel "Porgy." Gershwin wrote the opera "Porgy and Bess."

These three houses, 94-90 Church Street (1730, c. 1760, c. 1809) are good examples of the evolution of the Charleston single house. In the typical 18th-century single or double house, drawing rooms were on the second floor. There often was an office on the street level. The door to the piazza leads to the family entrance. Piazzas are turned to catch cooling breezes that blow in from the sea.

Tradd Street, many houses in this street were built during Colonial times.

Rainbow Row, East Bay Street. Most of these houses were built from the mid- to late-18th century. Originally they were directly on the water.

Old Exchange Building & Provost Dungeon, 122 East Bay Street, open to the public. Built between 1767 and 1772 as the Custom House and Exchange.

Waterfront Park

Evening view of Broad Street. St. Michael's lost its weather vane in Hurricane Hugo.

Pink House, 17 Chalmers. Built in 1712 as a tavern. The tile roof is characteristic of early Charleston.

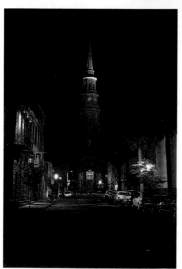

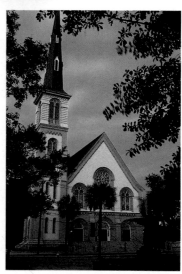

In order to attract more settlers, Charles Towne was advertised by the Lord Proprietors as tolerant to all religions. By 1700, Anglicans, Huguenots, Quakers, Baptists, Jews, Presbyterians and many more independent religions worshipped peacefully within the city. The city extended then between Cooper River and Meeting Street, the northern boundary was Market Street, in the south it was a creek near today's Water Street. The main street was present-day Church Street.

French Huguenot Church, built 1844-45. Huguenot refugees fleeing religious persecution under Louis XIV in France, established this congregation in the 1680's.

Dock Street Theater, 136 Church Street. Built inside the shell of the once elegant "Planters' Hotel," near the site of the 18th century original Dock Street Theater. The inside is a replica of a 1730's London Theater.

St. Philip's Episcopal Church, built in 1835-1838 after the church burned down. The oldest church organization in Charleston. The first church on this site was erected 1710-1721. Two signers of the Declaration of Independence are buried in the West Cemetery.

Powder Magazine, 79 Cumberland Street, built in c.1712, open to the public. One of the first buildings erected in the old walled city. It serves as museum of the Colonial Dames of America in the State of South Carolina.

City Market

Market Hall, 188 Meeting Street. Market Hall has not changed since it was built in 1841 as shown in this painting by Charles J. Hamilton, painted c. 1872. The Confederate Museum is located on the upper floor.

Circular Congregational Church, 150 Meeting Street. The Circular Congregational Church was the first dissenting church in South Carolina (1681-1685). The first building of white brick was called the White Meeting House. Meeting Street takes its name from this title. This is the fourth church on this site.

Hibernian Society Hall, 105 Meeting Street, built 1840. The building serves as headquarters for the Hibernian Society, one of Charleston's benevolent organizations. Beautiful iron gate.

Gibbes Museum of Art, 135 Meeting Street. Houses a collection of American paintings, prints and drawings from the 18th century to the present. This portrait of Judith Smith (Mrs. James Ladson) was painted by John Wollaston in 1767.

Fireproof Building, 100 Meeting Street, by appointment. Built 1822-1827. Designed by Robert Mills, the first native-born professional architect of the United States. Now houses the offices and archives of the South Carolina Historical Society.

39

Dr. John Lining House, 106 Broad Street, private residence, probably built before 1715. Dr. John Lining made the first systematic weather observation with instruments in America.

John Stuart House, 106 Tradd Street, private residence. Built around 1772 by John Stuart who was King George III's Superinten-dent for Indian Affairs. He had to flee Charleston after the colonists discovered that he had tried to incite the Catawba and Cherokee Indians against the Colonials.

Sword Gates, 32 Legare Street.

Pineapple Gate, 14 Legare Street.

Charles Town's colonial houses were built in a distinctive architectural style derived from England, Barbados and the West Indies. All houses on this page are pre-Revolutionary. The Charleston "single house" (one room wide) and the Charleston "double house" (two rooms wide) were built in many different styles.

Mikell House, 94 Rutledge Avenue, private residence. This Italianate mansion was built in 1853 by a Sea Island cotton planter as a summer residence in order to escape yellow fever, malaria and the monotony of rural life.

College of Charleston, Randolph Hall, 66 George Street. Founded in 1770 and chartered in 1785, the College of Charleston is the oldest institution of higher education in South Carolina, and the 13th oldest in America. It was the first municipal college established in the United States. Now it is part of the South Carolina State College System.

The Charleston Museum, 360 Meeting Street, is the oldest museum in the United States, founded in 1773 and now housed in a modern complex. Outside is a full replica of the Confederate States submarine *Hunley*. Inside, more than 300 years of Charleston history can be seen.

Joseph Manigault House, 350 Meeting Street, open to the public. Gabriel Manigault designed this Adam-style house for his brother in 1803. Furnished in period furniture.

Aiken-Rhett House, 48 Elizabeth Street, open to the public, built in 1817. This Greek Revival house was the home of Governor William Aiken, Jr.

The Citadel, 171 Moultrie Street, was founded in 1842 as the Military College of South Carolina. Citadel cadets have been involved in every national conflict since the Mexican War. Also see the Citadel Museum, located on the campus, and the dress parade on Fridays during the college year.

Fort Sumter, open to the public. This man-made island/fort, at the entrance of Charleston harbor, was the site of the first Civil War military action. On April 12, 1861, Confederate troops at Fort Johnson fired the first shots of the war at the Union-occupied Fort Sumter.

USS Yorktown, Patriots Point Naval and Maritime Museum, on the Cooper River. Docked here are the aircraft carrier *Yorktown*, the destroyer *Laffey*, the submarine *Clamagore*, and the nuclear-powered merchant ship *Savannah*. All are open to the public.

Fort Moultrie, open to the public. The original palmetto log fort was started in 1776 and was only half completed when attacked by a British fleet on June 28, 1776. Colonel William Moultrie's men repelled the assault in one of the first decisive victories of the Revolution.

Magnolia Cemetery, historic cemetery on the banks of the Cooper River.

Charleston Harbor.

Spoleto Festival U.S.A. was founded in 1977 by Gian Carlo Menotti, Pulitzer Prize and Kennedy Center Award-winning composer-librettist-director, as the "New World" counterpart to the Festival of Two Worlds, held every year in Spoleto, Italy.

Angel Oak, is one of America's oldest and largest oak trees. Estimated to be about 1,500 years old, the tree's trunk has a circumference of almost 26 feet, and a limb spread of 151 feet. Open to the public.

Charles Towne Landing, is a park located on the site of the first English settlement in South Carolina. The eighty acres of gardens, lagoons, wilderness and animal forest include replicas of a Colonial Village and of a 17th century trading vessel.

Old Santee Canal State Park, Moncks Corner, is the site of America's first canal which connected the Santee River with the Cooper River and thus provided a direct outlet to Charleston Harbor. Visitors will find miles of boardwalks and trails to observe turtles, osprey, alligators and blue herons. Canoes are available for exploring. An Interpretive Center provides information on the history of the area.

Cypress Gardens, a lush semi-tropical park with thousands of azaleas, camellias, wildflowers and migrating birds.

Drayton Hall Plantation, was built between 1738 and 1742. This Georgian Palladian plantation house survived the Civil War intact. Rich in architectural details, is not furnished.

Magnolia Plantation and Gardens, has been the ancestral home of the Drayton family for over 300 years. It is composed of the plantation house, a petting zoo, a mini horse ranch, the Audubon Swamp Garden, a "Biblical Garden" and miles of trails and boardwalks.

Middleton Place, has been the home of several generations of Middletons. America's first formal landscaped gardens were laid out in 1741 to enhance the setting of the Tudor Mansion, of which only a wing survived the Civil War. The plantation consists of the famous gardens, an activity-filled stableyard and the Middleton Place House Museum.

Boone Hall Plantation, originally a cotton plantation of over 17,000 acres, has one of the most majestic avenues of moss-draped live oaks in the South. Original plantation buildings include nine 18th century slave cabins, built of bricks made on the plantation and the Gin House, used for processing cotton. In 1935 the original plantation was replaced with the present mansion.

チャールストン―過去と現在

1670年4月、英国人入植者の一団を乗せたフリゲート艦「カロライナ」号が、クーパー、アシュリーの両河川の形成する港に到着した。入植者たちは、オールド・タウン・クリークを見おろす低い崖の上に、最初の居住地を開いた。

カロライナ号は、カロライナ真正独占領主団が組織した遠征隊に加わって英国を出航していたが、7カ月にわたる航海中に、船団中の2隻が遭難していた。カロライナ領主団は、強大な政治力を持つ8人の英国人から成り、現在の米国ノースカロライナ州からフロリダ州に至る土地を英国王の勅許により下賜されていた。

アシュリー川を隔てた半島部は、木が生い茂り、風も涼しかったため、そちらに入植した者もあった。この地域は、昔住んでいたインディアンの残した牡蠣殻に因んで、ホワイト・ポイントまたはオイスター・ポイントと呼ばれた。

領主たちは、「チャールズ・タウン」と名付けられたこの植民地を、活気にあふれ、あらゆる宗教に寛容な土地として宣伝したため、入植者が急速に増えた。こうして移民を増やし、植民地の経済を刺激し、チャールズ・タウンを英国との主要貿易港とするのが、領主たちの狙いであった。

1690年代半ばに、チャールズ・タウンは米の輸出を始めた。米は、その10年程前にマダガスカルから輸入された作物で、農園主や米商人の中には、この作物のおかげで後に米国有数の富を築くものも出た。しかし、米の耕作や収穫には、力があり、しかもマラリアや黄熱病に強い労働力が必要であった。このため、チャールズ・タウンには、毎年何百人もの奴隷がアフリカ西部から連れてこられた。

1719年初め、領主たちは、植民地における一部の輸入税を却下し、通貨の発行を禁止し、さらに入植者に土地を与える方針を取りやめて、インディアンから取り上げた広大な土地の所有権を主張した。スペイン艦隊がカロライナ侵略の準備を進めているとの知らせに、チャールズ・タウン議会は、自らを英国王保護下の新政府と宣言したため、領主たちによるサウスカロライナ統治は終りを告げた。

英国王直轄植民地となったチャールズ・タウンは、しばらく繁栄を続けた。クーパー川に突き出た8つの埠頭には、毎年500隻を超える外洋船が入ってきた。1740年代に入ると、奴隷たちの反乱、ヨーロッパで9年間続いた戦争による輸出減、そして家屋約300戸、埠頭・要塞数カ所を焼失する「1740年の大火」などの災難が続いたが、戦争が終わると、貿易活動は以前にも増して活発化した。英国の繊維産業の急成長で染料の需要が増大したため、平野地帯の農園主たちが新たに栽培を始めた藍は、いくら生産しても間に合わないほどだった。

1770年代には、カロライナ産の作物の価格は急騰し、チャールズ・タウンの港の年間輸出入量は、ニューヨークの港を凌ぐまでになった。裕福な市民は豪邸を新築し、夫人たちは、最新のロンドン・ファッションを身につけて観劇・舞踏会・音楽会などに出かけ、トーマス・エルフの高級家具で住まいを飾った。また、息子たちは海外に留学したり、家庭教師による教育を受けた。チャールズ・タウンでは、新聞が3紙発行され、米国南部唯一の書籍店兼製本所ができて、市民に情報・知識を提供した。

1776年6月28日、米国大陸会議がフィラデルフィアで、英国からの独立問題の討議を続けているさなかに、英軍艦9隻がサウスカロライナ沿岸のサリバン島の要塞を攻撃した。しかし、この艦隊は撃退され、チャールズ・タウンは無事だった。その4カ月後、チャールズ・タウン政府は米国独立宣言を承認した。独立戦争の戦場は主に米国北東部に集中しており、ボストン、ニューヨーク、フィラデルフィアを通過する貿易に支障が出たため、チャールズ・タウンに入港する船が、これまで以上に増えた。1779年、英国は、ワシントンの率いる米軍にてこずり、米国南部を攻撃すれば貿易を遮断できると考えて、チャールズ・タウンに大規模な陸海混合部隊を派遣した。42日間にわたる包囲攻撃の末、米国でただ1カ所開いていた海港チャールズ・タウンも英軍に明け渡された。英国軍によるチャールズ・タウン占領は2年半続いた。

1783年、サウスカロライナ州議会は、チャールズ・タウンの名称を「チャールストン」と変えて、英国王からの独立を宣言した。3年後、同議会は、州都を平野地帯から内陸に移すことを決議した。平野地帯の議員らの大反対を押し切って実現した新州都は、後にコロンビアと呼ばれるようになった。

19世紀に入る頃には、米に代わって藍が、主な輸出作物としての地位を急速に伸ばしていた。また、1791年には150万ポンドだったサウスカロライナ州の綿生産高は、その10年後には2,000万ポンドに増加していた。19世紀初めのナポレオン戦争後のヨーロッパで綿の需要が急増したため、綿農園主は巨万の富を築き、沿岸の島に大邸宅を建てたり、町に夏の別荘を建てたりした。

1824年、南部で初めての医科大学、サウスカロライナ医科大学が開校した。1842年には、士官学校ザ・シタデルが設立された。また、チャールストン市の公立学校は、授業料を無料にし、州内で最も優秀な公共教育制度を確立した。

1860年12月、160名の州議会議員たちが、米国連邦からの脱退を決議するためコロンビア市に集まったが、天然痘の大流行のため、会議の場をチャールストンに移さねばならなかった。決議の結果、160対0で、サウスカロライナ州の連邦脱退が決まった。南部連邦大統領となったジェファーソン・デイビスは、ボーレガード将軍を、チャールストンで南軍の指揮に当たらせた。

北軍のアンダーソン少佐は、サウスカロライナの戦略上の要地サムター砦に軍隊を進めたが、南軍が砦を明け渡さないため、サムター砦の攻撃を開始した。これが南北戦争（1861-65年）の幕開けである。北軍による海からの猛攻撃に、チャールストンは4年間近くにわたって果敢に対抗したが、シャーマン将軍率いる北軍が州都コロンビアに迫り、チャールストンへの供給路が絶たれようとしていたため、1865年2月17日夜、ついに南軍兵士たちは撤退。チャールストンは陥落して、廃墟の町が残った。

戦後の経済復興には時間がかかったが、破壊された鉄道や焼失した市街が少しずつ再建されて行った。チャールストン大学の研究者2名が、川岸で採れるリン酸塩で肥料が作れることを発見し、チャールストンの経済発展に貢献した。19世紀末の約25年間は、

大きな変化の時期となった。港の近代化、電話線の敷設、自転車という新しい発明品の導入、トロリー電車による交通の便の向上、砕いた貝殻を敷いた道路に代わる板石や花崗岩の舗装道路などが、次々と実現した。さらに、チャールストン市は、不衛生な屋外便所に代わる近代的な下水設備の設置という、最も急を要する大事業を開始した。

1920年に、先見の明のあるチャールストン市民たちが、米国でも初めての歴史保護運動を始めた。彼らが設立したチャールストン歴史保護協会の働きで、多くの歴史的建造物が破壊を免れた。

人種差別の時代から、法による平等の時代への移行は、穏やかという訳には行かなかったが、チャールストンでは、優れた黒人・白人指導者たちの努力で、サウスカロライナ州でも初めて公立高校や市営施設における人種差別を廃止し、警官などの市職員に黒人を採用するようになった。

この20年程の間に、チャールストン港は大きく発展し、米国東岸随一のコンテナ港となった。また、チャールストン市の中央ビジネス街も、チャールストン・プレースができて賑わいを増した。毎年チャールストンで開催される芸術・音楽祭スポレト・フェスティバルは、世界中から大勢の参加者を集めている。

USニューズ・アンド・ワールド誌1985年11月号で、チャールストン市は、「全米で最もビジネスに適した74都市」の一つに選ばれている。

1989年9月21日の真夜中近く、最大風速220km、高さ4-5mの高波を伴うハリケーン「ヒューゴ」が、チャールストンと周辺の海岸地区を襲った。沿岸の島々は水浸しになり、住民に避難命令の出たチャールストン市内では、木が根こそぎ倒れ、家々の屋根が飛び、煙突や塀が崩れるなどの被害が出た。商店のウィンドーもガラスが粉々に割れ、道路に溢れる濁流が流れ込み、1階はすべて泥に覆われてしまった。しかし、チャールストンは、300年の歴史を通じていつもそうしてきたように、災難の翌日には、もう町中が力を合わせて再建に立ち上がったのである。

Index — Charleston

LEGEND: Interesting and fun for children of all ages.

Access for handicapped people.

Partial access and/or with assistance.

Area Code 803

Tour #1: DOWNTOWN

TOUR #2: CITADEL, HISTORIC FORTS, NAVAL MUSEUM

Go north on Ashley Avenue, turn left on Moultrie Street, or go north on Lockwood Blvd. then follow signs to

Go US 17 N across Cooper River, after bridge exit SC 703, turn right at sign and go 1 mile to

Page 48

Citadel Museum
171 Moultrie Street
Tel.: 792-6846
Hours: Sun.-Fri. 2-5, Sat. 12-5
Dress parade Fridays 3:45 during school year.
Admission: Free

Page 50

Patriots Point Naval and Maritime Museum
Mount Pleasant
Tel.: 884-2727
Hours: Daily 9-6 (winter 9-5)
Admission: Yes

Return to SC 703, continue 10 miles to Sullivan's Island, turn right on West Middle Street to

49 Fort Sumter

Tour boats leave daily for a two-hour tour from City Marina, Lockwood Boulevard, at 9:30, 12, 2:30 (summer) and from Patriots Point at 10:45, 1:30, 4:00 (summer).
Handicapped-accessible tour boats at City Marina.
Tel.: 722-1691

51 Fort Moultrie, Sullivan's Island
Tel.: 883-3123
Hours: Daily 9-6 (winter 9-5)
Admission: Free

TOUR #3: ANGEL OAK, CHARLES TOWNE LANDING

Go US 17S, take SC 171 then SC 700, turn left onto SC 20 (at store), go approx. 2 miles to sign turn right to

Go US 17S across Ashley River, after bridge take SC 61N, go two miles, take SC 171, go 1 mile to

Page 56

Angel Oak
Tel.: 559-3496
Hours: Daily 9-5
Admission: Yes

Page 57

Charles Towne Landing
Tel.: 556-4450
Hours: Daily 9-6, (winter 9-5)
Admission: Yes

TOUR #4: OLD SANTEE CANAL STATE PARK, CYPRESS GARDENS

Take I-26 West (13.5 miles) to exit 208, turn right onto US 52, go 10.7 miles to turn-off to Cypress Gardens, follow signs. For Old Santee Canal State Park continue on US 52 (18 miles) to Moncks Corner, stay on US 52W, go 1.3 miles turn right and follow signs (2 miles) to

Page
58 Old Santee Canal State Park
900 Stony Landing Road, Moncks Corner
Tel.: 899-5200
Hours: Daily 9-6 (winter 9-5)
Admission: $3 per car

Page
59 Cypress Gardens
3030 Cypress Garden's Road
Monck's Corner
Tel.: 553-0515
Hours: Daily 9-5
Admission: Yes

TOUR #5: PLANTATIONS

Take US 17S across Ashley River, after bridge, take SC 61N, go 9 miles to

Page
60 Drayton Hall
3380 Ashley River Road
Tel.: 766-0188
Hours: Daily 10-5 (winter 10-3)
Admission: Yes

Continue on SC 61 for 1 mile to

61 Magnolia Plantation and Gardens
Ashley River Road
Tel.: 571-1266
Hours: Daily 8-Dusk, Ticket sales end at 5:30
Admission: Yes

Continue on SC 61 for 4 miles to

Page
62 Middleton Place
Ashley River Road
Tel.: 556-6020
Hours: Daily 9-5
Admission: Yes

Take US 17N across Cooper River (7 miles), turn left and follow sign to

63, 64 Boone Hall Plantation and Gardens
Long Point Road, Mount Pleasant
Tel.: 884-4371
Hours: Mon.-Sat. 8:30-6:30 (winter 9-5),
Sun. 1-5 (winter 1-4)
Admission: Yes

PUBLIC BEACHES

Folly Beach County Park
(US 17S, then SC 171 East)
West end of Folly Beach, Ashley Ave.
Tel.: 762-2172
Hours: Daily 10-7, (winter 10-5)
Showers, restrooms, vending area, lifeguards, dressing area
Admission: $3 car

Beachwalker Park
(US 17S, SC 171/SC 700, then SC 20)
Southwestern end of Kiawah Island
Beachwalker Drive
Tel.: 762-2172
Hours: Daily 10-7, (winter closed)
Showers, restrooms, snack bar, lifeguards, dressing area
Admission: $3 car

Sullivan's Island, Folly Beach and Isle of Palms are public beaches but no facilities. Swim at own risk.

CALENDAR OF EVENTS

(For other events please call 722-8338)

Festival of Houses
March - April
Tel.: 723-1623

Annual House & Garden
Candlelight Tours
September - October
Tel.: 722-4630

Spoleto Festival
May - June
Tel.: 722-2764

Moja African American Arts Festival
October
Tel.: 724-7309

Christmas in Charleston
December
Tel.: 853-8000

Information Centers:

Preservation Society, Visitors Center
"Dear Charleston: The Motion Picture"
147 King at Queen Street
Tel.: 723-4381
Hours: Mon.-Sat. 10-5, Sun. 1-5
Hourly showing daily

Charleston Visitor Center
375 Meeting Street
Tel.: 720-5678
Hours: Daily 8:30-5:30 (winter 8:30-5)

Historic Charleston Foundation
Preservation Center
108 Meeting Street
Tel.: 724-8484
Hours: Mon.-Sat. 10-5, Sun. 2-5

BOOKS BY CITIES IN COLOR, INC.

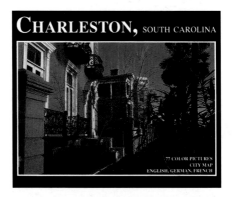

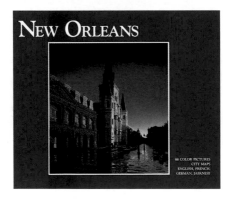

SAVANNAH
To be published in 1993

Also Available:
Vienna, Austria
Rio de Janeiro, Brazil

Cities in Color, Inc.
Lisa D. Hoff
12 Braemore Drive, N.W.
Atlanta, GA 30328-4344
Tel.: 404 255-1185 • Fax: 404 252-7218